Insects
Mosquitoes

Leo Statts

Launch!
An Imprint of Abdo Zoom
abdobooks.com

abdobooks.com

Published by Abdo Zoom, a division of ABDO, PO Box 398166, Minneapolis, Minnesota 55439.
Copyright © 2019 by Abdo Consulting Group, Inc. International copyrights reserved in all countries.
No part of this book may be reproduced in any form without written permission from the publisher.
Launch!™ is a trademark and logo of Abdo Zoom.

Printed in the United States of America, North Mankato, Minnesota.

092018
012019

THIS BOOK CONTAINS
RECYCLED MATERIALS

Photo Credits: AnimalsAnimals, iStock, Shutterstock

Production Contributors: Kenny Abdo, Jennie Forsberg, Grace Hansen, John Hansen

Design Contributors: Dorothy Toth, Neil Klinepier

Library of Congress Control Number: 2018945595

Publisher's Cataloging-in-Publication Data

Names: Statts, Leo, author.

Title: Mosquitoes / by Leo Statts.

Description: Minneapolis, Minnesota : Abdo Zoom, 2019 | Series: Insects |
    Includes online resources and index.

Identifiers: ISBN 9781532125096 (lib. bdg.) | ISBN 9781641856546 (pbk.) |
    ISBN 9781532126116 (ebook) | ISBN 9781532126628 (Read-to-me ebook)

Subjects: LCSH: Mosquitoes--Juvenile literature. | Bloodsucking insects--Juvenile
    literature. | Insects--Behavior--Juvenile literature. | Insects--Juvenile literature.

Classification: DDC 595.77--dc23

Table of Contents

Mosquitoes

Mosquitoes are insects. A group of them is known as a swarm. There are more than 3,000 known species of mosquitoes.

Body

Mosquitoes have two wings and six legs.

They have two **antennae** and two eyes.

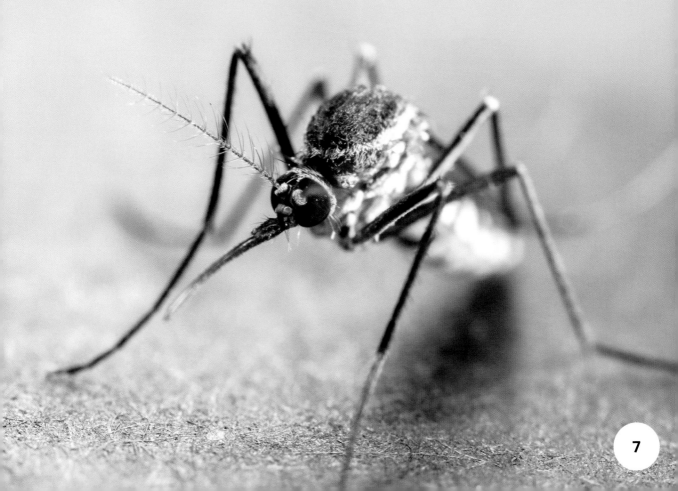

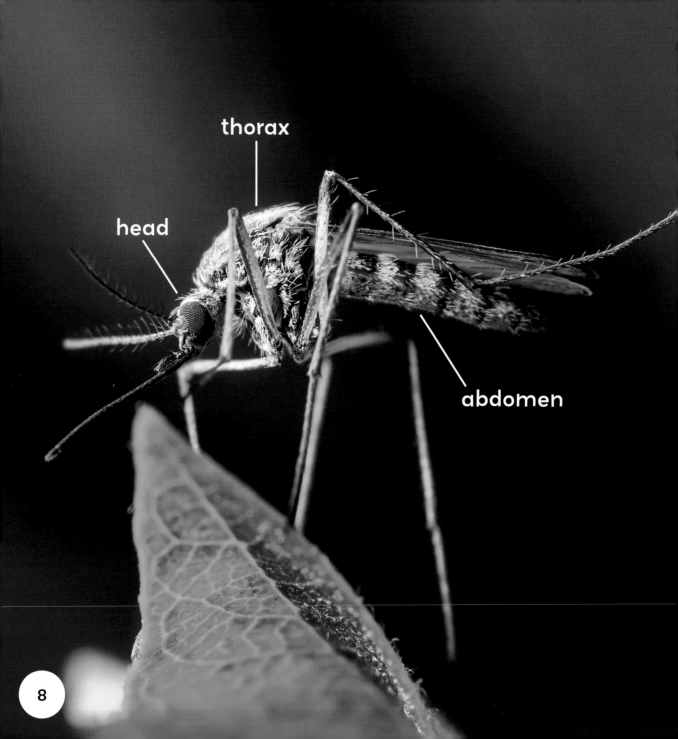

thorax

head

abdomen

Mosquitoes have three main body parts. They have a head, **thorax**, and **abdomen**.

Mosquitoes can be found almost anywhere on Earth. They often live near ponds and lakes.

Mosquitoes are food for many other animals and insects.

Food

All mosquitoes eat plant juices and nectar.

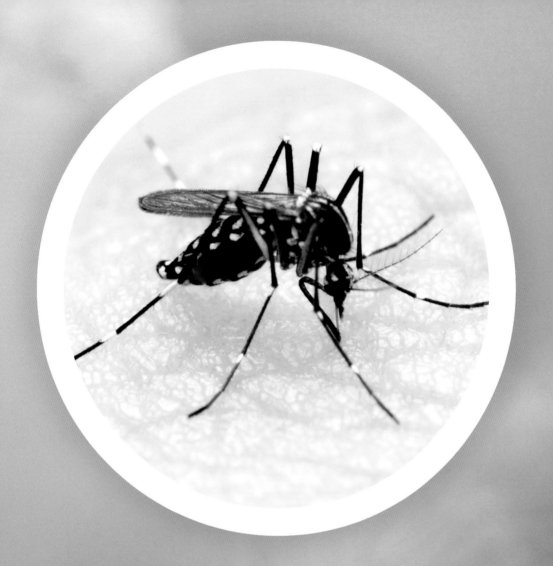

Only female mosquitoes drink blood.

A mosquito has a special **mouthpart** that looks like a straw. It bites humans and animals to drink their blood.

Life Cycle

Female mosquitoes lay their eggs on the surface of water.

It can take about two weeks for the eggs to become adult mosquitoes.

Mosquitoes can live between two weeks and six months.

Average Length

A mosquito is shorter than a penny.

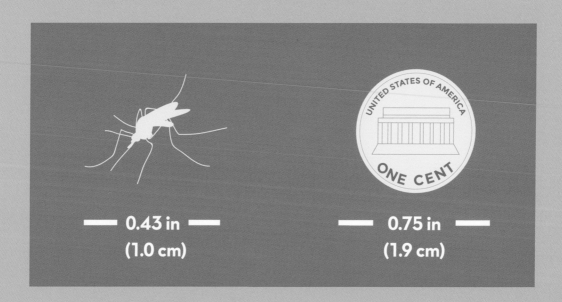

0.43 in
(1.0 cm)

0.75 in
(1.9 cm)

Average Weight

A mosquito is lighter than a quarter.

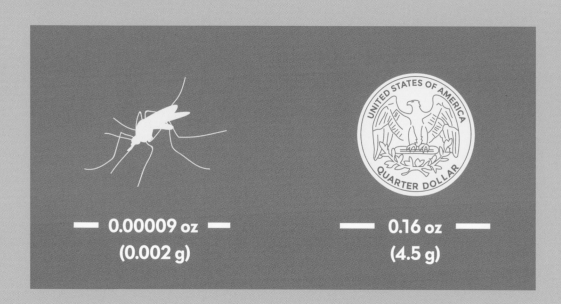

0.00009 oz
(0.002 g)

0.16 oz
(4.5 g)

Glossary

abdomen – the back part of an insect's body.

antennae – the two long, thin "feelers" on an insect's head.

mouthpart – a mouth shape that is specifically suited for grasping, biting, or sucking.

nectar – a sweet liquid, or sugar water, that flowering plants make.

species – living things that are very much alike.

surface – the top of a body of water.

thorax – the middle part of an insect's body.

Online Resources

For more information on
mosquitoes, please visit
abdobooklinks.com

Learn even more with the
Abdo Zoom Animals database.
Visit **abdozoom.com** today!

Index